BUSES OF WILTSHIRE AND DORSET
PAST AND PRESENT

Richard Stubbings

AMBERLEY

First published 2024

Amberley Publishing
The Hill, Stroud
Gloucestershire, GL5 4EP

www.amberley-books.com

Copyright © Richard Stubbings, 2024

The right of Richard Stubbings to be identified
as the Author of this work has been asserted in
accordance with the Copyrights, Designs and
Patents Act 1988.

ISBN 978 1 3981 1736 5 (print)
ISBN 978 1 3981 1737 2 (ebook)

British Library Cataloguing in Publication Data.
A catalogue record for this book is available from
the British Library.

Origination by Amberley Publishing.
Printed in the UK.

Introduction

My series of books covering past and present operations in the West Country continues with this second volume on Wiltshire and Dorset, the real gateway to this wonderful part of the country. Both counties are largely rural, featuring open chalk uplands. Their economies are mostly built around agriculture and tourism, although there is also a significant military presence, especially in Wiltshire around Salisbury Plain. There is industry, particularly around Swindon in the north of Wiltshire, where a number of national and international organisations are based. Swindon is, of course, also the home of God's Wonderful Railway, aka the Great Western. The county has just one city, medieval Salisbury, whose fourteenth-century cathedral boasts the tallest church spire in the country. The county town is Trowbridge. The largest centre of population in Dorset is in the south-east of the county, taking in the towns of Bournemouth, Poole and Christchurch. The county town is Dorchester, and along with the seaside resort of Weymouth these make up the other main towns. Dorset is also one of the few counties in the United Kingdom that has no motorways running through it.

As far as buses are concerned, like most of the West Country, Wiltshire and Dorset were firmly Tilling territory. Large areas of Wiltshire, especially around Swindon, came under the Bristol Omnibus Company. Moving further south the Wilts and Dorset Omnibus Company, based in Salisbury, served the south of Wiltshire and north of Hampshire. In 1963 it came under the control of the neighbouring Hants and Dorset Omnibus Company, which dominated the coast from Southampton along to Bournemouth and Poole and on towards Swanage. Moving westwards, most of Dorset was served by Southern National, and later Western National. The only municipal operations in these two counties were Swindon Corporation, which became Thamesdown Transport, and Bournemouth Corporation, latterly Yellow Buses. There were also local independent operators such as Bere Regis and District, although there were not a vast number of these.

With privatisation all of this changed. Bristol Omnibus was split between three new companies, Bristol Cityline, covered in a previous book, Badgerline and the Cheltenham and Gloucester company. Western National served only Cornwall and part of Devon and will be covered in a future volume. Hants and Dorset was divided up with a reformed Wilts and Dorset serving a much larger area. The rest of Hants and Dorset went to Hampshire Bus and then Stagecoach, and also to the reformed Provincial company, and are beyond the scope of this book; they will be covered in a future series on south-east operators. The operating area that served Dorset (and Somerset) came under the new Southern National. The current position for the area covered in this book is that the former Bristol operations around Swindon are now with Stagecoach West. The former Southern National operations in Dorset are now under First Hampshire and Dorset. Wilts and Dorset is now with Go South Coast.

The area's two municipal operations, Swindon and Bournemouth, were pretty much confined to their own urban areas for a long time. During the 1980s, Bristol Omnibus and Alder Valley, based in Reading, both withdrew a number of rural services in Wiltshire and Berkshire, although the latter isn't covered by this book. Thamesdown Transport stepped in and replaced a number of these rural services, resulting in their vehicles being seen over a much wider area. In 2017, the company was taken over by Go South Coast, trading as Swindon's Bus Company. This does make Go South Coast the unifying feature of this book, serving the whole of the area covered, from Swindon to Weymouth.

Bournemouth Transport was sold by the council in 2005, initially to the French-owned company Transdev. That firm merged with Veolia and subsequently RATP, also a French-owned company and operator of most of the public transport network around Paris, took over Bournemouth's operation. In 2019, Bournemouth Transport was sold in a management buyout, but sadly ceased trading completely at the beginning of August 2022. Their operations always remained mostly confined within the urban area of south-east Dorset. It has to be said that Bournemouth is simply not the same without its yellow buses.

One thing I have always regretted is that, although I have been a bus enthusiast since I was a small child, I didn't start taking photos of them until I was into my early teens. When I did begin taking photographs, my first camera was an instamatic that cost about £5, and a number of cereal packet tops, and was not therefore exactly the height of photographic technology. As such, I must apologise for the poor quality of some of the older photos, but I have decided to include them in this book for their historic relevance. However, this does mean that a number of vehicle types which I recall in service I never got to record on film. I have nevertheless included within this book some of the vehicles that I remember from my childhood but which have now entered preservation. However, I have not included any preserved vehicles if I have no recollection of those vehicles actually plying their trade in the liveries in which they are preserved and illustrated. I have also included photos taken from outside Wiltshire and Dorset as coaches do tend to roam further afield! Hence the presence of photos taken, for example, in Truro.

Something I have noticed is that since privatisation it can get incredibly complicated working out who is owned by whom, and how the different companies got to where they are now. On this front, Wikipedia has been a very helpful source of information, as has the excellent *Buses* magazine. I must thank my partner Debs for her support and help in preparing this book, reading through the drafts and checking them, making sure I've numbered the captions correctly, and also for the use of some of her photos in the book.

I'm starting this book off in the north of the area covered, in Swindon. We used to pass through Swindon regularly on our way from Somerset to see family in Cambridge. It was a long journey in pre-motorway days, but buswise a very interesting one! I saw Swindon Corporation vehicles regularly, but never photographed them. I feel justified therefore in including this shot of Northern Counties-bodied Daimler CVG6 145, JAM 145E. There were three in the batch, numbered 144–146, and they were the only front-loader CVG6s Swindon bought, and the last half-cabs purchased by the company. 145 has been preserved in corporation livery by Go South Coast. In this shot, however, it was owned by Thamesdown Transport as part of their heritage fleet and is seen at a rally at Newbury Racecourse in 2012.

In late 1977 a trip to Swindon produced 1961 Roe-bodied Daimler CVG6 115, XHR 115, of the Thamesdown Transport fleet, on Fleming Way with the bus station in the background. This vehicle was still wearing the old Swindon Corporation livery, the fleet becoming Thamesdown Transport as part of the local government reorganisation in 1974. 115 survived until 1978 when it was withdrawn from service.

Sporting the new Thamesdown livery was similar Daimler CVG6 123, XMW 123, also dating from 1961. A corporation-liveried CVG6 can be seen on the opposite carriageway, together with two Daimler Fleetlines, one with an ECW body and one with an MCW body.

In 1975, Thamesdown received a single batch of ECW-bodied Bristol RESLs. Pictured here is 167, JMW 167P. Previous batches of single-deckers had been on AEC and on Leyland chassis. This bus stayed in Swindon until 1987 when it migrated north to Tyneside to work with Blue Bus Services.

After the Daimler CVG6s, Swindon turned to the Daimler Fleetline for its double-decker requirements, initially with Northern Counties bodies, then one batch with MCW bodies. It finally settled on ECW bodywork as seen here on vehicle 201, BMR 201V, on Fleming Way, in late 1993.

Thamesdown also took advantage of the opportunity to buy some second-hand Fleetlines from Greater Manchester PTE. Thamesdown 218, TWH 698T, a Northern Counties-bodied example, formerly 6939 in the Manchester fleet, is seen near the bus station in 1993.

When the Fleetline went out of production Thamesdown decided upon the Dennis Dominator, its first examples being four with, unusually, single-deck Marshall Camair 80 bodies fitted with coach seats. The third of the batch, numbered 3, FAM 3W, is seen here, not in Swindon but in Paris Street Coach Station, Exeter, working on hire to National Express, an interesting choice of vehicle for this purpose.

Thamesdown's first new double-deck Dennis Dominators had Northern Counties bodies, as seen here on number 60, A60 WMW, laying over on Fleming Way in 1994. Behind it is another former Greater Manchester Fleetline, number 217, BVR 89T, again with Northern Counties bodywork.

Thamesdown also bought second-hand examples of the Dominator. 238, NRR 106W, also with a Northern Counties body, is an ex-Derby Corporation example, seen in the bus station in 1993 with more Thamesdown vehicles in the depot behind.

Another example of a second-hand Dominator is vehicle 235, PRE 37W, carrying an East Lancs body. This example was new to East Staffordshire District Council at Burton-on-Trent and was bought from Stevensons after they took over the East Staffordshire operation.

Thamesdown's last Dominators arrived in 1990 with an East Lancs-bodied batch, including 71, H971 XHR, seen here in the bus station. The bodywork on this vehicle makes an interesting comparison with the former East Staffordshire vehicle in the previous picture.

In 1993, Thamesdown's first Dennis Darts, carrying Plaxton Pointer bodies, arrived. 104, K104 OMW, is seen here on Fleming Way soon after delivery in 1993, on a wet and miserable day. Dennis Darts, particularly in the Dart SLF version, became the backbone of the fleet throughout the late 1990s and into the 2000s.

As well as the brand-new Dennis Darts, Thamesdown also took some second-hand Dennis Falcon Hs with Duple Dominant bodies. This chassis was closely related to the Dennis Dominator, although it was never that common a vehicle with less than 150 being built. They were often used on country services with Thamesdown, as here with Falcon H 11, XJF 91Y, a former Leicester vehicle, bought in 1987, leaving Swindon for Cirencester. Thamesdown's services expanded into rural areas during the 1980s to replace services withdrawn by Bristol Omnibus and Alder Valley.

Other Duple Dominant-bodied Dennis single-deckers that entered the Thamesdown fleet were three Dennis Lancets from Merseyside PTE. Seen here is former Merseyside 7030, EKA 230Y, now 30 in the Thamesdown fleet, in the bus station. Less than a hundred Lancets were built, and a third of these were exported. Merseyside had the largest fleet of these in the UK, with ten examples. Behind can be seen another former East Staffordshire Dennis Dominator, vehicle 232, LBF 232V.

Thamesdown did operate a small number of coaches. Leyland Tiger 305, A305 AHR, fitted with Duple Laser body, was new in 1984 and is seen here in the bus station on driver training duties. Sadly, this vehicle was lost in a fire in 1994.

In 2017, Thamesdown Transport was sold to the Go-Ahead Group and rebranded as Swindon's Bus Company. Here Optare Versa 402, WX60 EEA, is seen passing the bus station on 26 April 2022. A large number of Swindon's Buses carry names, 402 being *King George VI*. On my last visit to Swindon in November 2022, these vehicles were not in evidence.

Bound for the Great Western Hospital, Wright Solar-bodied Scania 526, WX59 GJK, is seen on 26 April 2022 having been delivered new to Thamesdown Transport. 526 carries the name *Balaklava*.

East Lancs Omnidekka-bodied Scania 372, YN55 NHE, *Earl of Dartmouth*, seen here leaving the bus station on 26 April 2022 on a private contract working, was formerly London United SLE11 before moving to Swindon in 2013.

Swindon's Bus Company 276, HF20 CVH, an Enviro 200MMC, is named *Western Leviathan*. All the vehicles of this batch have been named after the diesel hydraulic locomotives of the Western Class, which became Class 52, used on the Great Western mainline during the 1960s, 1970s and 1980s.

Seen here is is 363, SN51 AXW, an elderly Plaxton President-bodied Dennis Trident in the fleet of Swindon's Bus Company. New to Lothian Buses in 2001, it came to Thamesdown in 2015 and is seen parked in the bus station on 26 April 2022. 363 is one of the vehicles in the fleet that does not carry a name.

Dual-purpose Bristol RELHs in the Bristol Omnibus fleet carried this very smart reversed livery in pre-NBC days. 2062, WHW 374H, carries the yellow and red fleet number plate signifying allocation to Stroud Depot, so it was probably a fairly frequent visitor to Swindon. It is seen here at the Brislington Bus Rally on 31 July 2022. I used to ride on these vehicles sometimes between Wells and Bath, and splendid machines they were!

Bristol Omnibus was a late convert to rear-engine double-deckers, their first examples, for Bristol city services, not arriving until 1972. The first Bristol VRs for country area services arrived in 1975. Delivered in 1977, brand-new Bristol VRT 5521, PEU 516R, is seen on Fleming Way. Unsurprisingly, Bristol opted for the green option when the NBC imposed its corporate livery style, with the exception of buses of the former Cheltenham District fleet which went red.

The successor to Bristol Omnibus was Swindon & District. With privatisation of the NBC in 1983, the Bristol Omnibus operations in Gloucestershire were transferred to the Cheltenham & Gloucester Omnibus Company. In 1985, the NBC added Swindon & District to this and in 1986 this was all transferred to Western Travel. In 1990 the first new double-deckers arrived in the form of five Alexander-bodied Leyland Olympians. Seen here in the bus station is 101, G101 AAD.

A less usual vehicle to join the Swindon & District fleet was former Greater Manchester Leyland Titan 108, GNF 8V, which reached Swindon via South Midland. Outside London they didn't really achieve any success, although Reading bought a small number. As the bus operations in London were split up and different groupings came into being, so former London Titans did appear around the country, cascaded to the regional fleets. Greater Manchester bought a total of fifteen of these vehicles.

A contrast with the Bristol Omnibus Bristol VRT is Swindon & District 222, TWS 906T, formerly Bristol 5125. Delivered new to Bristol's Lawrence Hill Depot in 1979, it was transferred to Gloucester in 1981 and on to Swindon in 1982; it was converted from dual-door in 1987. It is pictured leaving Swindon bound for Wootton Bassett.

New to the Swindon & District fleet was 801, K901 OMW, a Wright-bodied Mercedes-Benz 811D. In 1993 Swindon & District succumbed to the stripes of Stagecoach.

The successor to Swindon & District is Stagecoach West. The Alexander ALX400-bodied Dennis Tridents must by now be the oldest double-deckers still in service with Stagecoach. 18177, MX04 XFV, seen departing the large bus station on service 7 to Highworth on 26 April 2022, was new to the Stagecoach operation in Manchester.

Here, wearing Stagecoach Gold livery, is Enviro 400MMC 15344, YP67 XBT, leaving the bus station for Royal Wootton Bassett on 26 April 2022. Stagecoach Gold vehicles carry leather seats, free Wi-Fi and increased legroom.

Alexander Dennis Dart SLF Pointer 2 34838, VU06 HZX, is seen here on 26 April 2022 about to enter the bus station on a local service. The Darts with the Alexander Dennis Pointer 2 bodies are now a diminishing breed in the Stagecoach fleets.

Enviro 400 15974, YP14 GZD, based on the Scania N230UD chassis, seen here leaving the bus station on 26 April 2022 bound for Cirencester, is in the second standard Stagecoach Group livery.

Swindon's Bus Company is now part of Go South Coast, as is Salisbury Reds. The latter's Enviro 400 1502, HF59 FAJ, is seen arriving in Swindon on service X5 from Salisbury via Marlborough on 26 April 2022. The journey across Wiltshire must be a very attractive one when seen from the top deck.

Swindon is an important calling place on the National Express network. BV17 GUG, from the Edwards of Avonmouth fleet, is seen on 26 April 2022 working service 401 to London from Bristol. A Volvo B11RT, it carries the National Express standard Caetano Levante body.

The major coach operator in the Swindon area is Barnes Coaches, originally based in the village of Aldbourne. Bova Futura WIB1444 was new to the company as H622 FUT, and is seen here, not in Swindon, but rather on a private hire to Hampton Court on 3 June 2000.

Barnes Coaches was established in 1920. Their current livery is this eye-catching all-over green, seen here on Irizar i6 YN18 ZNP, photographed in Swindon Bus Station on 14 November 2022. Their vehicles are a common sight all over the country on extended tours.

Trowbridge was originally a Western National garage, before passing to Bristol Omnibus in 1970. Coach-seated Bristol SUL4A number 420, 270 KTA, dating from 1962 was a Trowbridge-based vehicle during the late 1960s. It has since been preserved and is seen here at the Tavistock Running Day in 2018.

While Bristol FLF 2019, 824 KDV, was not a Trowbridge-based vehicle, others from this 1963 batch were. These vehicles fitted very neatly into the Bristol Omnibus fleet when operations were transferred. The former Western National FLFs were easily distinguishable from the native Bristol examples by virtue of their side-by-side destination displays, the Bristol company's own examples having the T-type display.

Bristol MW 2934, 924 AHY, delivered in 1958, was a Trowbridge-based vehicle and is typical of the many examples of the type that were the mainstay of so many country routes all over the Bristol Omnibus area. They are a type I rode on frequently to and from school in Somerset. Thankfully, it is another example that made it into preservation and is seen here in Winchester.

With privatisation, Bristol Omnibus operations passed to Badgerline and consequently to First Group, formed when the Badgerline Group merged with the GRT Group, based in Scotland. First West of England's operations in Trowbridge are considerably less than Bristol's, with the services working from their Bath Depot. Wright Solar-bodied Scania L94 65724, LK55 ABZ, is seen working service 265 to Warminster on 26 February 2018. This vehicle has since passed to First Kernow at Camborne Depot.

In 2018, Trowbridge town services were operated by Frome Minibuses, as seen here with Optare Solo VX56 NAA, working service 66 to Longfield on 26 February. This company is now known as Frome Bus.

Seen pausing at the bus stop in Market Street, Trowbridge, on 26 February 2018 is Faresaver Enviro 200 PX12 COH. New to the fleet of Reay's of Wigton, it joined the Faresaver fleet in 2017 and is working their X34 Chippenham to Frome service.

Bus services from Bath into west Wiltshire towards Warminster and on to Salisbury were rebranded as Discover, receiving this special, route branded livery. The successor to service 265 pictured earlier is service D1 seen here on 17 November 2022 in the hands of Wright Eclipse Urban 2-bodied Volvo B7RLE 69506, BJ11 XHY. A slightly tenuous link back to Bristol Omnibus days can be seen in the Volvo's registration letters XHY, HY formerly being a Bristol mark, but now of course merely a random selection of letters.

By 2022, Faresaver had become the major operator in Trowbridge. They took over a number of town services from Frome Buses, including the 66 seen earlier. In this view, it is in the hands of Optare Solo SR YJ66 AOA, formerly in the fleet of West Midlands operator Go igo.

Another operator working into Trowbridge is Young of Radstock, which trades as C. T. Coaches. Their Optare Solo YK05 CAO is in Fore Street, arriving on service 185 from Hallatrow on 17 November 2022. This vehicle was new to Owen of Denbigh, arriving with C. T. Coaches in 2015 from M. & H., Trefnant.

Chippenham didn't have a Bristol Omnibus depot but rather was an outstation of Trowbridge, with vehicles staying at the bus station overnight. A Trowbridge Bristol MW that probably spent some of its time based outstationed in Chippenham was 2969, 981 EHY, delivered in 1959. Seen here in preservation carrying the very smart Bristol Omnibus one-person livery and wearing Bath Services fleetnames, by the time of its transfer to Trowbridge it carried NBC green. Bristol MWs in this livery would have been a frequent sight in the Chippenham area.

Bristol Omnibus 8335, UHY 383, is typical of the Bristol country area Bristol KSWs, this one dating from 1955, that served towns such as Chippenham. Their ECW bodies were fitted with platform doors to provide a bit more comfort on the interurban routes that they operated. This example is seen in preservation at the bus rally in Chippenham on 21 May 2017.

Bristol Omnibus vehicles allocated to Bath carried the Bath Services fleetname for a long time. L8515, 969 EHW, a 1959 Bristol LD-type Lodekka, was allocated to Bath and would probably have been a frequent visitor to Chippenham during its working life. It is seen here in Chippenham at the bus rally there on 13 May 2018, displaying route number 465 for the Bath to Swindon via Chippenham service. Two vehicles from this batch were based in Wells when I was at school, and I rode on them regularly.

Chippenham Bus Station would once have been a sea of Tilling green and cream, then a sea of NBC green, followed by a sea of Badgerline yellow and green. Their successor, First West of England, no longer operates to Chippenham, and the bus station is now a sea of white and purple vehicles from the Faresaver fleet. It was a very wet day on 14 November 2022 when Enviro 200 LX10 AUR was seen leaving the bus station for Bath on service X31. This vehicle was new to Docklands Buses in London.

Seen at the other end of the X31 route, in Dorchester Street, Bath, and setting out on its return to Chippenham, Alexander ALX400-bodied Volvo B7TL, LJ54 BDX, was new to Arriva London North, moving to Faresaver in 2016. Seen here in January 2018, it has since left the fleet.

Faresaver's double-deck fleet now consists entirely of Volvo B9TLs with Wright Eclipse Gemini 2 bodies. RRU 345, new to Centrewest in London as LK59 CWR, is seen here leaving the bus station for Frome on service X34 on that very wet 14 November 2022.

Optare Solos also feature in the Faresaver fleet, as seen here with YE52 BUS. New to Veolia in South Wales as CN07 KZJ, it arrived with Faresaver in 2014 from Aston of Worcester and is photographed here on a Chippenham town service on 10 October 2019.

New to the now defunct fleet of GHA, Ruabon, YJ15 AYF, is an example of the Optare Solo SR. On 14 November 2022 it was laying over in Chippenham Bus Station.

Links to Swindon are now provided by Stagecoach West's service 55, using Enviro 400MMCs in route-branded Stagecoach Gold livery. 15347, YP67 XPW, is seen here on 10 October 2019.

Another Chippenham operator with a white and purple livery is Coachstyle of Nettleton. Leaving, at that moment, an otherwise deserted Chippenham Bus Station on 14 November 2022 is YJ14 BWF, an Optare Solo SR new to the company in 2014.

Wilts & Dorset and Hants & Dorset became part of the National Bus Company and in 1972 were merged under the Hants & Dorset name and adopted the NBC's red livery rather than the green, which might have been expected. Bristol VR 3429, GEL 679V, is seen in the bus station in Endless Street in about 1984, preparing to leave for Woodfall.

Wilts & Dorset also undertook some work on behalf of National Express. In the early 2000s the variety of vehicles used on National Express work was wider than it is now. Seen at Heathrow Airport on 9 August 2000, and included here as it is heading for Salisbury is Bova Futura 3211, L211 CRU.

With the privatisation of the NBC the Wilts & Dorset name re-emerged and in 1987 the firm was sold in a management buyout. DAF became the single-decker of choice, although in small quantities. Seen here is DAF SB220-based Optare Delta 3506, L506 AJT, also in Salisbury Bus Station. This was the last of the only batch of Optare Deltas bought by the company.

MCW and Optare Metroriders (or MetroRiders for the Optare model) were a popular choice with Wilts & Dorset, with many examples joining the fleet, both new and second-hand from the Trent fleet. Two Optare examples, 2525, K525 UJT, which was new to the fleet, and 2238, P238 CTV, formerly Trent 1238, stand together in Salisbury Bus Station on 28 March 2002.

When the Optare MetroRiders ceased production, Wilts & Dorset turned to the Optare Solo. 2628, S628 JRU, enters Salisbury Bus Station bound for Romsey on 28 March 2002.

Longer distance services were often in the hands of coaches such as DAF SB3000 3215, R215 NFX, carrying a Plaxton Premiere 320 body and arriving from Bath on an X4 working on 28 March 2002.

Wilts & Dorset also added second-hand coaches to their fleet for use on those longer distance services. B278 KPF, a Leyland Tiger with Plaxton Paramount 3200 2 body, was new to the Garston Garage of London Country for Green Line work. It is seen here in Salisbury Bus Station on 28 March 2002, bound for Romsey.

Seen on Blue Boar Row on 28 March 2002 is Optare Excel 3605, X605 XFX, in a dedicated livery for a Park & Ride service, sponsored by Wiltshire County Council. Four Excels were delivered in 2000 specifically for the Salisbury Park & Ride.

The former Hants & Dorset operations were by now in the hands of Stagecoach Hampshire Bus. Alexander-bodied Volvo Olympian 279, P279 VPN, is seen on 28 March 2002 arriving in Salisbury from Andover.

Seen on the same day and on the same route is Hampshire Bus 607, L427 TJK, a Volvo B10M with Alexander PS body, wearing Stagecoach's second standard livery. This is very much a standard vehicle choice for Stagecoach, which built up a large fleet of these reliable buses.

Go South Coast 4752, R752 GDL, a Volvo Olympian with Northern Counties Palatine 1 body, began life on the Isle of Wight with Southern Vectis. That firm was taken over by Go South Coast in 2005 and in 2009 4752 moved across the Solent to join the Wilts & Dorset fleet at Salisbury. It is seen on Blue Boar Row on 2 September 2016, just a few months before the final disappearance from service of step-entrance double-decker buses.

Go South Coast use a number of different fleetnames. This East Lancs Olympus bodied Scania, HF08 TKX, is numbered 8101 in the Tourist fleet, which is a coaching operation. Seen on Blue Boar Row on 2 September 2016, it is operating a local journey although, as its livery indicates, it was more normally to be found on the Stonehenge Tour.

Bristol Omnibus long operated a service to Salisbury from Bath. At one time this route would have featured Bristol KSWs fitted with platform doors, such as L8089, OHY 938, a 1952 low-bridge example from the Bath Services fleet, seen here at a bus rally in Taunton on 8 May 2016.

Bristol's successor, First West of England, sadly does not have any Bristol KSWs, so on 2 September 2016 they would have had this Scania with Wright Eclipse Solar body, seen here, as usual, on Blue Boar Row, LK55 ACJ, numbered 65726 in their fleet.

Dorset County Council operated this Optare Versa, YJ60 KFW, on service 20 to Salisbury from Blandford Forum. It is seen on Blue Boar Row on 2 September 2016. The route is now worked by Damory, part of Go South Coast. This vehicle has since passed to Centrebus and is now working around Leicester.

By 2019, the East Lancs-bodied Scanias used on the Stonehenge Tour from Salisbury had been replaced by Enviro 400MMCs, and the livery had changed to green. It is also now operated by Salisbury Reds rather than Tourist. 1635, HF66 CFD, is seen on 2 January 2019 in New Canal, Salisbury.

As noted previously, the Bath to Salisbury service 265 was rebranded under the Discover name in 2018, along with other routes working into Wiltshire from Bath, and renumbered D1. The vehicles were given a dedicated livery, seen here on vehicle 69508, BJ11 EBX, a Volvo B7RLE with Wright Eclipse Urban 2 body on Blue Boar Row on 2 January 2019.

In 2003, Wilts & Dorset became part of the Go-Ahead Group, and now works as Go South Coast, as noted previously. The Go-Ahead Group have a large number of Scania OmniCity double-deckers spread around their different fleets. Seen in Blue Boar Row on 6 June 2022, 1138, HF09 BJX, carrying the fleetname 'Salisbury Reds', is awaiting departure to Larkhill on Salisbury Plain.

Also sporting the name 'Salisbury Reds', used on vehicles based in Salisbury, Enviro 400 1506, HF59 FAU, stands on Blue Boar Row, also awaiting departure to Larkhill on 6 June 2022. Salisbury's bus station in Endless Street closed in 2014 and Blue Boar Row in the centre is now very much the hub of bus operations with most services terminating there.

Another Enviro 400, this time with the 'More' fleetname, and in a much brighter livery, 1537, HJ63 JJV, is on service X3 to Bournemouth on 2 September 2016.

Another Enviro 400, another livery! Salisbury Reds 1607, HF65 AYA, is seen approaching its terminus on an X7 working from Southampton, wearing a smart dedicated livery for the route on 6 June 2022.

Enviro 200 2727, HF65 AYG, seen again on 6 June 2022, is in the newer, brighter livery for the Salisbury Reds vehicles than the deeper red seen earlier.

The year 2022 was important in the life of the country with the first ever Platinum Jubilee, celebrating the seventy-year reign of Elizabeth II. A number of firms painted vehicles in special liveries to celebrate the occasion, including Stagecoach South. Their Enviro 400MMC 10699, SN66 VVK, is seen arriving in Salisbury on an Activ8 working from Andover on 6 June 2022.

Stagecoach South also operate into Salisbury via Winterslow on service 87. Andover-based Enviro 200 36027, GX07 HUU is also seen on 6 June 2022, on Blue Boar Row.

Damory is another fleet within the Go South Coast operation. Enviro 200 2766, YX17 NHU, is leaving for Blandford on service 20 on 6 June 2022.

Bournemouth was a favourite holiday destination of my grandfather. As it was somewhat closer to our home in Somerset than his home in East Anglia, we used to go and see him while he was there. Bournemouth Corporation was unusual for a South of England operator in that from 1969 it standardised on Alexander bodywork for its double-deckers. Leyland Atlantean 232, ORU 232G, is seen here in Gervis Place in around 1975. This vehicle was one of the first batch of seventeen such vehicles to join the fleet.

Showing small detail differences on its Alexander body to the previous picture, Leyland Atlantean 259, ULJ 259J, is seen at Bournemouth Pier, again in around 1975 and was delivered in 1971, a member of the third batch of such vehicles.

In 1973, Bournemouth started a town centre service, using small-capacity vehicles. Seen here in 1975 is M4, OLJ 404M, one of two Bedford VAS3s with Strachan bodies bought specifically for the service.

From 1973 Bournemouth standardised on the Fleetline double-decker, still with Alexander bodywork, to their AL design. A later vehicle, from 1980, 158, ERU 158V, is seen here in Gervis Place on 21 June 1989 bound for the Bloomfield Estate.

After the Fleetline went out of production, Bournemouth bought a single batch of Leyland Olympians with, unusually, Marshall bodies. These were the only Olympians that Marshall ever supplied the bodies for. 192, TJT 192X, is seen in Gervis Place on 21 June 1989.

Bournemouth next turned to Volvo for its double-deck requirements, buying a number of B10M-50 Citybus chassis fitted with Alexander RV type bodies. Vehicle 214, F214 WRU, was laying over in Bournemouth Square on 21 June 1989 when just two months old.

Like so many seaside towns, Bournemouth had a long history of operating open-top buses. Alexander AL-bodied Leyland Fleetline 138, VJT 138S, is seen here in the mid-1990s at Bournemouth Pier. I remember well rides on Bournemouth's open-toppers out to Hengistbury Head during family holidays.

A livery alteration in the early 1990s saw a blue roof and skirt applied, as seen here with Leyland Fleetline 165, GRU 165V, fitted with the usual Alexander AL body and rounding Bournemouth Square on 24 June 1992.

A busy scene in Bournemouth Square on 31 August 2000 as Fleetline 170, MFX 170W, carrying the usual Alexander AL body and one of the final batch of Fleetlines, heads off to Stourvale Estate.

Also in Bournemouth Square on 31 August 2000 was Marshall-bodied Leyland Olympian 180, TJT 180X, bound for Westbourne. This bus had recently received a repaint to apply the blue roof and skirt.

After a couple of batches of Volvo Citybuses in 1988 and 1989, Bournemouth turned to Dennis and a batch of Dominators with East Lancs bodies. Number 264, H264 MFX, is in Bournemouth Square on 31 August 2000, heading for Somerford.

Bournemouth bought a single batch of Dennis Lances with East Lancs EL2000 bodies. In case anyone was wondering, vehicle 402, L402 BFX, is not heading for the Channel Islands but rather an area of Bournemouth near Poole!

Bournemouth followed this one batch of Dennis Lances with its first Dennis Darts, again fitted with East Lancs EL2000 bodies. 458, M458 LLJ, is seen here, again in Bournemouth Square, en route to Christchurch.

The low-floor era arrived in Bournemouth with a batch of Dennis Dart SLFs carrying East Lancs Spryte bodies. 477, R477 NPR, is in Bournemouth Square on route 6 to Kinson on 31 August 2000.

Low-floor double-deckers arrived in Bournemouth with a batch of East Lancs Lolyne-bodied Dennis Tridents. 274, T274 BPR, is in Bournemouth Square on 31 August 2000, drawing attention to its low-floor credentials.

Bournemouth has maintained a coach fleet for some years, under the name Yellow Coaches. Unsurprisingly, they could crop up all over the country, as in the case of DAF MB230 9, RIB8749, originally registered H399 MFX and carrying a Plaxton Paramount 3500 III body. It is seen here on a trip to Penzance.

Another member of the Yellow Coaches private hire fleet was this Irizar Century-bodied Scania, 341, R341 LPR, seen at Guildford Cathedral on 19 May 2001. The coach in Leger Holidays livery behind was also a Yellow Coaches vehicle, 323, P323 ARU, a Berkhof Axial-bodied Volvo B10M.

Bournemouth has been a contractor to National Express for some years. Seen at Bournemouth Station on 31 August 2000 is Van Hool Alizee T9-bodied Scania 383, W383 UEL, bound for Poole on NX 035 from London.

Family holidays to Milford-on-Sea in the early 1970s meant sometimes being treated to a ride into Bournemouth with Hants & Dorset, normally either a Bristol KSW or a rear-entrance Bristol FS such as 1450, 5677 EL, dating from 1961, seen here at the 2017 Alton Rally. Hants & Dorset was the only firm I can remember who fitted these sun visors over the windscreens on their Bristol Ks and on the rear-entrance Lodekkas. I don't recall ever seeing them on the Bristol FLFs.

In 1971, Hants & Dorset took delivery of six Roe-bodied Daimler Fleetlines diverted from the Gosport & Fareham Omnibus Company, which traded as Provincial, receiving six dual-door Bristol RELLs instead. All six Fleetlines were allocated to Poole, and were delivered in Tilling green and cream. Seen here at a bus rally in the 1990s is 1901, VRU 124J. These vehicles were the first rear-engined double-deckers in the fleet, the first Bristol VRs not arriving until 1973.

Bournemouth Bus Station, 1975, with Hants & Dorset 629, RFE 461, a former Lincolnshire Road Car Bristol MW demoted from coach work and transferred to the south coast in 1973 and wearing the white and black discs signifying allocation to Bournemouth Depot. This vehicle was withdrawn from service in 1977.

Laying over in the large parking area in the centre of the bus station, Hants & Dorset Bristol LH 3558, GLJ 490N, is another Bournemouth-based vehicle.

Hants & Dorset Bristol LH 3538, ORU 538M, makes an interesting comparison with the previous picture as it is one of the LHs with a cut-away front allowing it to access the Sandbanks Ferry without grounding when working on service 7 to Swanage.

Leyland National 3619, NEL 862M, seems to be attracting some closer inspection judging by the chap behind it kneeling on the ground examining something! In the background, right to left, are another Sandbanks LH, an early, dual-purpose RELL, and two more LHs, one still wearing Hants & Dorset green and cream.

Brand-new Poole-based Bristol VRT 3322, JJT 434N, is seen here with some of the old order, a Bristol LD still in Tilling green and cream, an LH also in Tilling green and cream, an FLF in NBC red and a training vehicle, as well as a Sandbanks LH.

In the central parking area, this smart Bristol RELH, vehicle 1051, AEL 6B, was used on holiday tours, despite it being painted in the NBC's local coach livery. Sadly, this fine vehicle was one of many that was lost in the disastrous fire that destroyed Bournemouth Bus Station in 1976.

During 1972, Hants & Dorset purchased a number of Willowbrook-bodied Leyland Panthers from Maidstone & District to help speed up the introduction of one-person operation. Seen in Bournemouth in around 1975 is former Maidstone 1689, JKK 189E, now numbered 1694, and still wearing the dark-green livery of its former operator.

With the privatisation of the National Bus Company, Hants & Dorset's operations around Bournemouth passed to the newly reformed Wilts & Dorset company. Former Hants & Dorset Bristol RELL 622, XLJ 727K, seen here in Avenue Road, Bournemouth, on 21 June 1989, is still wearing NBC red and white local coach livery. These vehicles never carried the new privatised livery of red, white and black.

Wilts & Dorset needed additional double-deck capacity and purchased a number of former London Transport DMS-type Daimler Fleetlines. This MCW-bodied example, 1945, KUC 935P, arrived via South Wales Transport and is seen in Bourne Avenue, Bournemouth, on layover before returning to Poole on 21 June 1989.

Wilts & Dorset also bought a number of MCW-bodied Bristol VRs from West Midlands PTE in 1987. 3461, GOG 636N, formerly West Midlands 4636, is seen here on Avenue Road, Bournemouth on 21 June 1989.

The more usual NBC standard ECW-bodied Bristol VR is exemplified here by Lymington-based 3456, KRU 856W, photographed in Gervis Place on service 121.

Wilts & Dorset also bought a number of second-hand Leyland Olympians in the late 1980s and early 1990s. Seen leaving Bournemouth for Wimborne on 14 March 1992 is Roe-bodied example 3919, A159 FPG, formerly LR59 in the London Country fleet and based at Harlow.

Pictured in Gervis Place, Bournemouth, on 24 June 1992 is former West Yorkshire PTE 5070, CUB 70Y, a Roe-bodied Leyland Olympian, now 3911 in the Wilts & Dorset fleet, and now also a convertible open-topper.

The DAF DB250-based Optare Spectra became Wilts & Dorset's standard double-decker during the 1990s. Here the company's very first, 3101, K101 VLJ, is seen in Bournemouth Square on 31 August 2000, heading back to its home town of Poole. In total, Wilts & Dorset operated seventy-eight Spectras, making it the largest operator of the type in the country.

As already noted, Wilts & Dorset was a keen operator of the Metrorider, in both the original MCW form and the later Optare version. Seen here in Bournemouth Square in about 1991 is one of the first batch of MCW Metroriders, 2327, E478 MEL. New to Salisbury Depot in January 1988, it was soon transferred to Lymington, and then on to Poole in July 1988. It carries the name 'Skipper', used for minibus services.

Pictured here at Bournemouth Station on 31 August 2000 is MetroRider 2547, N547 UFX, one of the later Optare models. It is interesting to compare the detail differences between this and the MCW example pictured above.

Wilts & Dorset was the first operator to take the Optare Solo into service, eventually building up a fleet of eighty-five. 2610, R610 NFX, is seen here, again on 31 August 2000, at Bournemouth Station.

Optare Excel 3603, W603 PLJ, was the third member of the first batch of Optare Excels bought by Wilts & Dorset. It is seen in Bournemouth Square bound for Wimborne on 31 August 2000. The company eventually bought a total of fifteen of these vehicles.

When my partner and I attended the Bournemouth Rally on 3 July 2022 I realised I hadn't photographed the Bournemouth fleet in its days as a member of the RATP Group. Little did we realise that a month later Yellow Buses would cease trading completely so we never would manage to photograph them. Yellow Buses 5035, GX09 ZZS, was a second-hand addition to the fleet. A Volvo B9TL with Wright Eclipse Gemini 2 body, this vehicle previously served with Isle of Man Public Transport and carried the Isle of Man registration JMN 51R.

Another second-hand acquisition was this former Tower Transit Enviro 200, YX12 AEU, becoming 2026 in the Yellow Buses fleet, seen again at the Bournemouth Rally in 2022. The yellow used latterly was a brighter shade than the original primrose employed in Bournemouth Corporation days.

Second-hand purchases seemed to be the general rule in the company's latter days. This Enviro 400MMC, SN65 OHZ, 4041 in the Yellow Buses fleet, came from Johnson of Henley-in-Arden.

Our trip to Bournemouth on 25 October 2022 found a very different bus scene. With the demise of Yellow Buses, Go South Coast subsidiary More stepped into the breach. Among the vehicles transferred in are a number of Unibus-liveried Enviro 400MMCs, such as 1672, HF69 CSV, seen here at Bournemouth Pier bound for Somerford. Seen in the background is an East Lancs Myllennium Vyking-bodied Volvo B7TL in More livery.

Another vehicle transferred to Bournemouth is this former Bluestar Enviro 400, 1254, LX54 ETR. New to London General as E47, it moved to Bluestar in 2020. It is seen here at Bournemouth Pier on service 1b from Christchurch.

Another service from Christchurch into Bournemouth is the 1a, seen here again at Bournemouth Pier, in the hands of Enviro 200MMC 249, HF18 CJJ.

Working in the opposite direction at Bournemouth Pier on 25 October 2022 was Enviro 400MMC 1673, HF69 CRV, heading for Wimborne.

This elderly Volvo B7TL, with convertible open-top East Lancs Millennium Vyking body, 1822 HF54 KXU, was heading back into Bournemouth on service 5 from Kinson, with Bournemouth Pier's sightseeing wheel behind it.

Arriving in the centre of Bournemouth on service 16 from Poole is 1198, HF58 GZN, one of a large number of Scania OmniCitys in the fleet. The lovely autumn hues of the trees and the bright sunshine made this a colourful scene on 25 October 2022.

Seen in Gervis Place on service m2 to Poole is Volvo B7RLE 2254, HF12 GVU, carrying a Wright Eclipse Urban 2 body, with a rear view of Scania 1198, now moving to work service 17.

There are still yellow buses in Bournemouth! This Volvo B9TL with Wright Eclipse Gemini 2 body, HF11 HCO, is in the fleet of Yellow Coaches, which was bought by Xelabus. Seen here, again in Gervis Place on 25 October, it is awaiting its departure time for a journey to Branksome.

Carrying the standard Xelabus livery, T3WSX is a Dennis Trident with Alexander ALX400 body that the company bought from Preston Bus. It was, however, new to London United as their TA279, carrying the registration LG02 FDV. It is seen in Gervis Place on tendered route 33 to Christchurch. Although it's not yellow, it is quite appropriate in a way as the Xelabus green and cream livery is a reminder of the other major operator in Bournemouth in years gone by, namely Hants & Dorset and their livery of Tilling green and cream, which in turn also brings back childhood holiday memories of rides on their Bristol KSWs, top deck, front seat!

There are also still open-toppers in Bournemouth. Go South Coast operate 'The Purbeck Breezer' service between Bournemouth and Swanage via Poole and Sandbanks. On 25 October 2022, Swanage-based 1701, HJ16 HTA, a Volvo B5TL with Egyptian-built MCV EvoSeti body, is seen, in Bournemouth Square, nearing the end of its journey.

Bournemouth's premier coach operator for many years was Excelsior, which operated an extensive programme of tours throughout the United Kingdom and Europe, and further afield. Their vehicles never carried any identification as to their manufacture and mostly carried EXC or XEL registrations, such as here on vehicle 516. A14 EXC is a Volvo B10M with Plaxton Premiere 320 body, seen parked in Truro on a tour of Cornwall.

In 2016 the Excelsior operation was bought by Go South Coast. The name was kept as one of their coaching brands, but the livery was changed to this attractive two-tone blue scheme, as modelled by vehicle 7838, A15 XEL. Seen at the 2022 Bournemouth Bus Rally, it is a Volvo B11R with Jonckheere JHV body, previously registered BP15 OLJ.

Wilts & Dorset retained its Bristol REs for a few years after privatisation. However, they kept their NBC dual-purpose livery, minus the logo. 620, TRU 947J, is seen in Poole Bus Station on 26 August 1989, hemmed in by double-deckers, thereby showing something of the double-deck variety in the fleet at this time. Going from left to right behind the RE are a Bristol VR in the post-privatisation livery, another VR in NBC livery, a former London Transport DMS Fleetline also in NBC livery and an Optare Spectra. This RE has since been superbly preserved in Wilts & Dorset's dual-purpose livery of Tilling red with a cream roof.

When London Transport decided to rid themselves of their large fleet of DMS-type Daimler Fleetlines Wilts & Dorset bought twenty, all with MCW bodies. Parked in Poole Bus Station on 26 August 1989 are 1907, OUC 45R and 1945, KUC 935P. 1945 arrived via South Wales Transport.

The journey from Poole to Sandbanks, and onwards to Swanage, has long been a regular route for members of the open-top fleet. Departing Poole Bus Station for Sandbanks on 26 August 1989 is Bristol VR 3351, OEL 232P.

Another DMS-type Fleetline to join the fleet was 1935, KUC 951P, seen here leaving the bus station for Canford Heath on 26 August 1989. Unlike the Fleetlines in the previous picture, this vehicle still wears NBC red and has NBC-style fleetnames, although without the logo. Its destination display has been altered from its London days and is also different to the one on the DMS it is passing.

As well as its Optare Spectras, Wilts & Dorset also bought a number of young DAF DB250 double-deckers from Wall of Sharston in Greater Manchester in 1997. 3152, N13 WAL, fitted with a Northern Counties Palatine 2 body, which Wilts & Dorset modified to convertible open-top, is seen leaving Poole Bus Station on 1 August 2001.

Wilts & Dorset also acquired some youthful DAF SB220 single-deckers from Wall of Sharston, near Manchester. Seen on 1 August 2001, 3509, N15 WAL, has a Hungarian-built Ikarus body which makes an interesting contrast with the stylish Optare Delta body on the same chassis seen earlier in Salisbury, being, I feel, a little more utilitarian looking.

Wilts & Dorset also bought a number of young second-hand Leyland Olympians, such as this Roe-bodied example, from West Yorkshire PTE. Some of these were also altered to convertible open-top, including 4912, EWY 80Y. However, when seen in Poole Bus Station on a hot 1 August 2001 it had its top firmly on!

Working into Poole on 1 August 2001, was Bournemouth Yellow Buses' East Lancs Spryte-bodied Dennis Dart SLF 475, R475 NPR. Despite being route-branded for Bournemouth's service 6, it was working to Poole Ferry on service 30.

Arriving in Poole on 1 August 2001, on a National Express service to Perranporth, is Plaxton Premiere 350-bodied Volvo B10M, P183 NAK, from the Truronian fleet. Only four years old, Truronian was already this coach's fifth owner. Lasting only about ten months with this firm, this coach would have three more owners before being exported to Zimbabwe in 2014.

Flightlink was a network of services, originally worked by Flights of Birmingham and later operated by National Express using vehicles from several different operators connecting various towns and cities with the airports. Seen here on 1 August 2001 is A7 XCL, a Volvo B10M with a Plaxton Paragon body from the fleet of Excelsior of Bournemouth, entering Poole Bus Station bound for Gatwick Airport.

Hants & Dorset bought a substantial number of young Bristol LHs from Bristol Omnibus in 1981 which subsequently passed to Wilts & Dorset on privatisation. Some of them received a modification involving cutting away part of the front of the vehicle to avoid them grounding when using the Sandbanks Ferry. 3854, AFB 590V, is seen here leaving Poole Bus Station on 26 August 1989 still in NBC red.

Seen the same day as the Bristol LH, Leyland National 3721, VFX 987S, is an example of the standard NBC types that were still in use at privatisation, and one that survived long enough to receive the new livery.

The only other operator in Poole at this time was Solent Blue Line. Their coach-seated all-Leyland Olympian 708, F708 SDL, is seen arriving at the bus station on 26 August 1989 from Southampton.

Wilts and Dorset became part of the Go Ahead Group in 2003. In 2006, operations in the south of England were grouped together as Go South Coast, with services in Bournemouth and Poole using the fleetname More. Enviro 200MMC 254, HF18 CJY, is seen here in the bus station on 13 June 2022.

Volvo B7RLE 2270, HF12 GWO, carrying Wright Eclipse Urban 2 body, is seen here on 13 June 2022 leaving Poole for the Royal Bournemouth Hospital. These Volvos and the Enviro 200MMCs seem to be the main types of single-decker currently in use in Poole.

Two Optare Solo SRs in Poole carry this dedicated livery for circular service 1. Numbered 3801 and 3802, they are registered BP09 ONE and PB09 ONE. The latter is seen here on 13 June 2022.

Open-toppers are still around in Poole. Seen heading for Sandbanks on 13 June 2022, Volvo B7TL 1822, HF52 KTU, carries an East Lancs Myllennium Vyking convertible open-top body.

Yellow Buses were still working into Poole and here their Volvo B9TL 5054, HF11 HCV, with Wright Eclipse Gemini 2 body, is seen passing the bus station on 13 June 2022. Yellow Buses stopped using Poole Bus Station in 2020.

Entering the bus station on 13 June 2022 is More 1406, HF59 DMO, a Scania N230UD with Optare Visionaire convertible open-top body.

Scania OmniCity 1142, HW09 BBU, is seen here, again on 13 June 2022, entering the bus station on the frequent service 60.

Arriving in Poole from Weymouth on the Jurassic Coaster service X54 from Weymouth is First Hampshire & Dorset Enviro 400 33726, SN12 AKY, looking very smart in its colourful dedicated livery.

National Express services do not go into the bus station now but rather use an open area in a car park next to it. In this view, taken on 13 June 2022, National Express Caetano Levante 3-bodied Scania BV69 KTG is shortly to leave for Heathrow Airport on NX 204.

Megabus Caetano Levante-bodied Volvo, B8R BK14 LFH, from the Yellow Coaches fleet, has just arrived in Poole from London, again on 13 June 2022. Just over a month later Yellow Buses and Yellow Coaches went out of business and this vehicle, the other coaches in the fleet and the Megabus operations passed to Xelabus. National Express took their own inter-city coach routes in-house.

Another of Wilts & Dorset's second-hand Leyland Olympians is this former North Devon Red Bus ECW-bodied example, 3907, A990 XAF. Formerly North Devon Red Bus 1819, it is pictured here at Swanage Station, the terminus of the attractive Swanage Railway. Like a number of second-hand double-deck additions to the fleet, this vehicle was altered to convertible open-top.

West Yorkshire PTE disposed of its Roe-bodied Leyland Olympians at a young age, and a number of them found their way to Wilts & Dorset. Again, they became convertible open-toppers. 3908, UWW 12X, is pictured at Swanage Station, awaiting departure for Bournemouth.

As mentioned previously, Wilts & Dorset purchased a number of young DAFs, both single- and double-deckers from Walls of Sharston near Manchester. DAF DB250 3148, M17 WAL, is seen here at Swanage Depot, next to Swanage Station. Its Northern Counties Palatine 2 body has been converted to a convertible open-topper. Pictured on 7 November 2009, it is probably not surprising that its top is firmly on! By now, Wilts & Dorset was a member of the Go Ahead Group.

Wilts & Dorset, now Go Ahead South Coast, also invested in new partial open-top buses like 1401, HF09 FVU. A Scania N230 with an Optare Visionaire body, it is seen at Swanage Station on 7 November 2009, when just five months old, awaiting departure to Bournemouth. The service was branded as the 'Purbeck Breezer', a name it still carries today, and the vehicles initially received this dedicated livery.

Also parked at Swanage Station on 7 November 2009, Optare Olympus-bodied Scania 1412, HF09 FVT, is lettered for the 'Purbeck Breezer' Swanage to Poole service.

'The Purbeck Breezer' would certainly have lived up to its name on a damp, breezy 10 November 2022 when MCV-bodied Volvo B5TL 1705, HJ16 HTA, was working the X50 service from Bournemouth to Studland.

Bound for Poole on service 40, closed top MCV-bodied Volvo B5TL 1701, HJ16 HSV, would have provided a slightly warmer journey on that breezy, damp 10 November 2022.

Shaftesbury is a lovely market town with a long history; it is where King Canute died in 1035 and also where the famous Hovis bread advert of the 1970s was filmed. It was an outstation of Wilts and Dorset's Blandford Depot and vehicles were kept in a car park near the town centre. It was also a convenient stopping point on my many journeys between Cornwall and Surrey. Such a trip in about 1995 found 3205, B205 REL, a Leyland Tiger TRCTL with Duple Laser 2 body laying over before its next duty.

Shaftesbury outstation on 31 March 2002 saw a cross-section of Optares parked up. Seen here are Optare Solo 2625, S625 JRU, Optare Delta 3506, L506 AJT and Optare Spectra 3145, M145 KRU.

Wilts & Dorset certainly developed a fondness for DAFs, purchasing a number of second-hand examples. Arriving from London Coaches in 2002 was this Van Hool Alizee-bodied DAF SB3000, 3220, M578 RCP. Allocated to Salisbury, it is seen here in Shaftesbury on 21 April 2003, laying over before returning to Salisbury on service 27.

Laying over in Fore Street, just by the town hall, Salisbury Reds Optare Solo SR 3818, HW62 CNV, has just arrived in Shaftesbury at the end of its journey from Salisbury on service 29 on a bright and sunny 17 November 2022. It makes an interesting contrast with the Van Hool-bodied DAF in the previous picture that was also used on the Salisbury service.

South West Coaches also work into Shaftesbury now with a couple of services, including the X2 from Gillingham. Seen soon after the Salisbury Reds' Optare had departed is Wright StreetLite DF BD20 ODK.

No book covering Dorset would be complete without a mention of Bere Regis & District. From their formation in 1929 they built up an extensive network of services around rural Dorset, eventually amassing a fleet of over eighty vehicles. The company ceased trading in 1995, their operations passing to the Cawlett Group, who owned Southern National, and who were in turn taken over by First Group. Seen here at its home depot in Dorchester is JFX 232N, one of four Bedford YRTs with elegant Plaxton Panorama Elite III bodies delivered in 1975, becoming the company's flagship vehicles for a time.

An interesting contrast in coaching style is provided here by Go South Coast's HF18 CKK. A Volvo 9700, it is a member of the Excelsior fleet and is seen in Dorchester on 11 August 2019.

Weymouth is a popular holiday destination and was very much the domain of Southern National in Tilling days. Under the National Bus Company, Southern National ceased as a separate entity, working under the Western National name until being revived after privatisation. Bristol VRT 603, LWG 846P, a former Yorkshire Traction vehicle, is seen here departing for Portland Bill in 1994.

Found resting in Weymouth Depot in summer 1994 were convertible open-top Southern National Bristol VRTs 934 and 942, VDV 134S and VDV 142S.

Wilts & Dorset worked into Weymouth from Bournemouth. Optare Spectra 3125, L125 ELJ, is laying over at The King's Statue. The statue of King George III on the sea front in Weymouth has for many years been the main terminal point for bus services in the town.

Smith of Portland competed with Southern National on the route to Portland Bill in the early 1990s with Bristol REs such as YHY 586J, seen in the summer of 1994. New to Bristol Omnibus, these buses were purchased from Western National, whose livery they actually still carried.

In 1999 Southern National became part of First Group, with the Weymouth operations joining First Hampshire and Dorset. Weymouth Garage on 3 March 2020 contained these three Volvo B7TLs with Alexander ALX400 bodies converted to partial open-top. 32031 and 32033 and possibly 32046 are branded for the Jurassic Coaster service.

Wearing its newer, more colourful Jurassic Coaster livery and laying over prior to departing on service X54 to Poole, First Hampshire and Dorset 37987, BJ11 ECX, is a Volvo B9TL with Wright Eclipse Gemini 2 body, seen on 3 March 2020. This has to be one of the most scenic bus services in the country.

Carrying 'Wessex' fleetnames, First Hampshire and Dorset Volvo B7RLE Wright Eclipse Urban 2-bodied 69553, BF12 KWM, passes The King's Statue on 9 May 2022, wearing route branding for local service 2 to Littlemoor.

Another Wright-bodied Volvo B7RLE, 69545, BF12 KWC, is one of the vehicles route-branded for service 10 to Dorchester. Here it is seen laying over at The King's Statue.

Wright StreetLite DF 63184, SN14 DXC, is seen here at The King's Statue on 9 May 2022 having just arrived from Portland on service 1. The DF refers to the entrance door being ahead of the front axle – 'door forward' as opposed to behind the axle – WF, 'wheel forward'.

Laying over at The King's Statue on 4 October 2022, 37582, HX08 DXK, is a Volvo B9TL with Wight Eclipse Gemini 2 body. It was working service 2 to Littlemoor, normally the preserve of route-branded Volvo B7RLEs.

The former Wilts & Dorset services into Weymouth are now operated by Go South Coast subsidiary Damory. Damory was a Blandford-based coach operator taken over by Wilts & Dorset in 1993. On 9 May 2022, service X12 from Blandford was being operated by Scania N230UB 2005, HF58 HTL.

Pimperne, near Blandford, is the home depot of Damory's Enviro 400 1507, HW62 CVF. Laying over at The King's Statue, it is working service X12 to Blandford Forum on 4 October 2022.

Bibliography

Crawley, R. J. and Simpson, F. D., *THE YEARS BETWEEN The Story of Western National and Southern National from 1929* (Exeter: Calton Promotions)

Curtis, Martin and Walker, Mike, *Bristol Omnibus Services – The Green Years* (Bath: Millstream Books, 2007)

Lyons, Mark, *The Go-Ahead Group* (Hersham: Ian Allan Publishing Ltd, 2012)

Macfarlane, Allan, *A Pictorial Tribute to the Bristol Omnibus Company and Associated Fleets 1936 – 1983* (Poole: Oxford Publishing Co.,1985)

Morris, Colin, *Southern National Omnibus Company* (Hersham: Ian Allan Publishing Company, 2007)

Witton, A. M., *Fleetbook 12 Buses of South West England* (Manchester: A. M. Witton, 1977–80)